A Literature Kit™ FOR

Curious George

• • • • • • • • • • • • • •

By H. A. Rey

Written by Marie-Helen Goyetche

GRADES 1 - 2

Classroom Complete Press

P.O. Box 19729
San Diego, CA 92159
Tel: 1-800-663-3609 / Fax: 1-800-663-3608
Email: service@classroomcompletepress.com

www.classroomcompletepress.com

ISBN-13: 978-1-55319-319-7
ISBN-10: 1-55319-319-9

© 2007

Critical Thinking Skills

Curious George

Skills For Critical Thinking	Chapter Questions					
	Phonics	Word Study	Comprehension	Reading Response	Writing Tasks	Graphic Organizers
LEVEL 1 Knowledge • Identify Story Elements		✓	✓			✓
• Recall Details	✓	✓	✓		✓	✓
• Match			✓			
• Sequence			✓			
• Recognize Basic Concepts	✓	✓				
LEVEL 2 Comprehension • Compare & Contrast			✓			
• Summarize			✓			
• Recognize Main Idea			✓	✓		
• Describe			✓		✓	
• Classify		✓	✓		✓	
LEVEL 3 Application • Plan					✓	
• Interview				✓		
• Make Inferences						✓
LEVEL 4 Analysis • Draw Conclusions				✓	✓	✓
• Recognize Cause & Effect				✓		
LEVEL 5 Synthesis • Predict					✓	
• Design					✓	
• Create					✓	
• Imagine Alternatives					✓	
LEVEL 6 Evaluation • Opinion				✓	✓	✓
• Make Judgements					✓	

Based on Bloom's Taxonomy

Contents

• • • •　•　• • • •　•　• • • •

FREE! 6 Bonus Activities!

3 EASY STEPS to receive your 6 Bonus Activities!

- Go to our website:
  www.classroomcompletepress.com\bonus
- Click on item CC2100 – Curious George
- Enter pass code CC2100D

Assessment Rubric

Curious George

Student's Name: _____ Task: _____ Level:_____

	Level 1	Level 2	Level 3	Level 4
Details	Student can give one detail from the story	Student can give two details from the story	Student can give three details from the story	Student can give four or more details from the story
Characters	Student refers to characters using he or she	Student refers to characters using the boy or the girl	Student refers to characters using names	Student refers to all characters using full names and titles
Information	Student gives incorrect information	Student gives mixed up information	Student gives literal information	Student gives correct information
Questions and Answers	Student cannot answer any teacher questions	Student provides some answers to teacher questions	Student provides correct answers to teacher questions	Student provides thoughtful responses to teacher questions

STRENGTHS:

WEAKNESSES:

NEXT STEPS:

Teacher Guide

Our resource has been created for ease of use by both TEACHERS and STUDENTS alike.

Introduction

his resource provides ready-to-use information and activities for beginning readers. It can be used in any Language Arts program to strengthen children's reading, writing and thinking skills. You may wish to use our resource on its own, or as part of a larger unit on the adventures of Curious George, a unit on monkeys, etc. It is comprised of interesting and engaging student activities in language, reading comprehension and writing, and can be used effectively for individual, small group or whole class activities.

How Is Our Literature Kit™ Organized?

STUDENT HANDOUTS

Activities in language, reading comprehension and writing (*in the form of reproducible worksheets*) make up the majority of our resource. There are six pages each of PHONICS activities, WORD STUDY activities, COMPREHENSION activities and WRITING tasks. All are either a half-page or full page long. Also provided is a six-page mini-booklet of READING RESPONSE activities. All of these activities contain words and/or phrases from the story which will help the students learn, practice and review important vocabulary words. The writing tasks and reading response mini-book provide opportunities for students to think and write both critically and creatively about the story. It is not expected that all activities will be used, but are provided for variety and flexibility in the unit.

- Also provided are two puzzles, a **word search** and **crossword**. Each of these worksheets can be completed as individual activities or done in pairs.
- Three **Graphic Organizers** are included to help develop students' thinking and writing skills (*see page 6 for suggestions on using the Graphic Organizers*). The **Assessment Rubric** (*page 4*) is a useful tool for evaluating students' responses to many of the activities in our resource. The **Comprehension Quiz** (*page 46*) can be used for either a follow-up review or assessment at the completion of the unit.

DISCUSSION QUESTIONS

It is a good idea to introduce a new story to students by preparing them for reading. Using a read-aloud approach, you may wish to open a discussion with the **Before You Read** Discussion Questions (*see page 9*) in the Teacher Guide. Then, read the story out loud. As you are reading, use the **As You Read** questions to engage the students in the story. Once you have completed the read-aloud and the students are familiar with the story, follow-up with the **After You Read** questions. You can present the After You Read questions orally for a continued whole group discussion, or write them on the chalkboard and have students discuss possible answers in small groups and then report back to the class.

PICTURE CUES

Our resource contains three main types of pages, each with a different purpose and use. A Picture Cue at the top of each page shows, at a glance, what the page is for.

 Teacher Guide
- Information and tools for the teacher

 Student Handout
- Reproducible worksheets and activities

 Easy Marking™ Answer Key
- Answers for student activities

EASY MARKING™ ANSWER KEY

Marking students' worksheets is fast and easy with our **Answer Key**. Answers are listed in columns – just line up the column with its corresponding worksheet, as shown, and see how every question matches up with its answer!

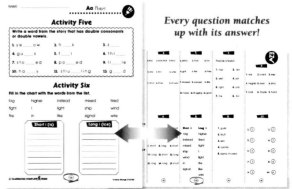

1, 2, 3
Graphic Organizers

The three **Graphic Organizers** included in this Literature Kit™ are especially suited to a study of *Curious George*. Below are suggestions for using each organizer in your classroom, or they may be adapted to suit the individual needs of your students. The organizers can be used on a projection system or interactive whiteboard in teacher-led activities, and/or photocopied for use as student worksheets. To evaluate students' responses to any of the organizers, you may wish to use the **Assessment Rubric** (*on page 4*).

MY FEELINGS

Use this organizer to help the children identify how they felt as certain passages were read. In the left-hand column, record the things that happened to George. In the right-hand column, the children are to write down how they felt as the event unfolded. This can be used for either independent work or as a whole class activity. As a whole class activity, record several different responses from the children. Then count and record how many students experienced each response (i.e., sad – 4, mad – 7, upset – 8). By looking at these numbers, you can get a sense of the different sub-groups' responses. Then use the numbers for a graphing activity in Math!

Found on Page 53.

SUM IT UP!

This organizer develops students' understanding of story elements. It can be used multiple times, each time with the students choosing different predicaments (problem situations) that George gets into. Here is a guide to help students identify the information needed for each of the questions:

Who are the characters involved in this event?
What happens, exactly? What is the problem? Give details.
Where does the event take place?
When does it happen?
Why does George get into this predicament in the first place?
How is the problem solved?

Found on Page 54.

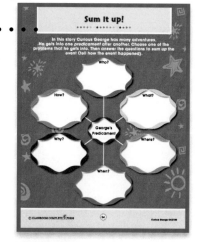

MIXED UP WORDS

This is an excellent activity to develop vocabulary and spelling skills. To make the activity more challenging, ask students to use only certain kinds of words from the story (for example, nouns and verbs). Or have the students choose certain words from the story and modify them before mixing them up (i.e., choose only singular nouns and change them to plural). This activity is perfect for use in pairs or as a whole class activity. As a whole class activity, use the graphic organizer with the answers covered. Have the students call out their answers.

Found on Page 55.

Bloom's Taxonomy* for Reading Comprehension

The activities in our resource engage and build the full range of thinking skills that are essential for students' reading comprehension. Based on the six levels of thinking in Bloom's Taxonomy, questions are given that challenge students to not only recall what they have read, but move beyond this to understand the text through higher-order thinking. By using higher-order skills of application, analysis, synthesis and evaluation, students become active readers, drawing more meaning from the text, and applying and extending their learning in more sophisticated ways.

This Literature Kit™, therefore, is an effective tool for any Language Arts program. Whether it is used in whole or in part, or adapted to meet individual student needs, this resource provides teachers with the important questions to ask, inspiring students' interest, creativity, and promoting meaningful learning.

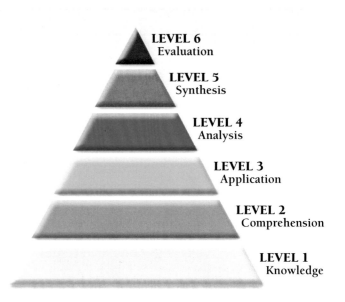

LEVEL 6 Evaluation
LEVEL 5 Synthesis
LEVEL 4 Analysis
LEVEL 3 Application
LEVEL 2 Comprehension
LEVEL 1 Knowledge

**BLOOM'S TAXONOMY:
6 LEVELS OF THINKING**

Bloom's Taxonomy is a widely used tool by educators for classifying learning objectives, and is based on the work of Benjamin Bloom.

Summary of the Story

This is the well-loved story about a curious little monkey, named George, who is caught in his home land of Africa by a man in a yellow hat. The man brings George to another continent to be placed in a Zoo. Inspired by his curiosity for the world around him, George has one adventure after another from the time he leaves Africa to the time he finally arrives at the Zoo. On the ship, George tries to fly like the sea gulls he sees, but this only gets him wet. He copies the man in the yellow hat by talking on the phone. He dials 1-2-3-4-5-6-7, which is the number for the Fire Department, and this phone call gets him in prison. The prison watchmen try to catch him, but he manages to escape by walking along the telephone wires. He sees a man with some balloons and wants one of them. However, he ends up with the whole bunch and finds himself flying through the air over the city's traffic. The man in the yellow hat has to pay for all the balloons. At the end of the story, George finally ends up in a tree at the Zoo. It was a nice place to live!

Vocabulary

Included in our Literature Kit™ are 20 vocabulary words from **Curious George** in the form of **word cards** (*pages 43 and 44*). The word cards may be used in a variety of hands-on activities. Also included is a page of 10 blank word cards that may be filled in with other words from the story, or words that fit in with a related subject or theme (*page 45*). You may wish to write the words on the cards or have the children add the words themselves.

Here are suggestions for hands-on activities using the word cards. Make photocopies of the cards for each student or for each group of students.

- Have the children classify the words by parts of speech (verbs, nouns, adjectives, etc.).
- Put the cards face down and have students pick 3 or 4 cards; they can write a story inspired by the cards they select (for example, a new adventure about Curious George).
- Combine and shuffle the vocabulary words with those from another story (perhaps another book by H. A. Rey, or another story about monkeys). Have the children categorize the words by story.
- Have the children use as many word cards as possible to write complete sentences. They will need to write more words on the blank cards (articles, prepositions, etc.)
- Have the children place the words in alphabetical order.
- Have the children work in pairs and each take half of the cards. Without saying the word, one child describes the word on the card, and the other student guesses what the word is.
- Put the cards face down and have students pick up a card and create a word web with it.
- Have the children cut up the words in syllables.

caught	curious	department	fascinated	fault
gulls	gust	harm	lightning	naughty
overboard	prison	promise	sailor	shore
signal	stool	struggling	watchman	whisk

············· Suggestions for Further Reading ·····················

BOOKS BY H. A. AND MARGRET REY
Curious George Goes to the Beach, © 1999
Curious George in the Snow, © 1998
Curious George Makes Pancakes, © 1998
Curious George and the Pizza, © 1998
Curious George Goes to School, © 1998
Curious George Visits the Zoo, ©1985
Curious George at the Fire Station, ©1985
Curious George Flies a Kite, ©1977
Curious George Gets a Medal, ©1974
Curious George Takes a Job, ©1974
Curious George Rides a Bike, ©1973
Curious George Learns the Alphabet, ©1973
Curious George Goes to the Hospital, ©1966

Discussion Questions

 Before You Read

1. The title of this book is *Curious George*. Do you think that the word *curious* is used in a positive or negative sense? Explain.

2. Look at the illustration on the front cover. How do you think the monkey feels about finding a yellow hat? Why do you think he feels this way?

3. The author of this book is H.A. Rey. What do you know about this author?

4. Do you think this will be a sad story? A funny story? A silly story? Explain.

As You Read

1. Why do you think the man wants to bring the monkey back to a Zoo?

2. Do you agree with the man capturing the wild monkey and taking him away? Why or why not?

3. How do you think the man knew that the monkey's name was George?

4. Why do you think George wants to: Fly like sea gulls? Use the phone? Have a balloon?

5. If the sailors had not thrown him a life belt, do you think George would have been able swim?

6. How would you have felt in George's place making all those mistakes?

7. How do you think the man knew that the large yellow straw hat would attract George?

After You Read

1. Do you think George will be happy at the Zoo?

2. Do you think the Fire Department overreacted when George played with the phone?

3. Why do you think George couldn't stop getting into trouble?

4. Do you want to read another adventure about George? Why or why not?

H. A. Rey (1898–1977) and Margret Rey (1906–1996)

Hans Augusto Rey and Margarete Elisabeth Waldstein (Margret Rey) were both born in Hamburg, Germany.

They got married on August 16, 1935 in Brazil but soon moved to Paris, France.

Hans published his first book called **Raffy and the Nine Monkeys**. In Britain and the United States this book was published as **Cecily G. and the Nine Monkeys**. One of the nine monkeys in this book was Curious George. The Reys felt that Curious George needed a book of his own. So Hans and Margret began writing stories about George.

At the end of the 1930's, Hitler and the Nazis were attacking France. On June 14, 1940, Hans and Margret escaped the invasion by only a few hours. They finally settled in Cambridge, Massachusetts.

Their publisher suggested not to use Margret's name on their books, although Curious George was written and illustrated by both. Later stories of George have both names on them.

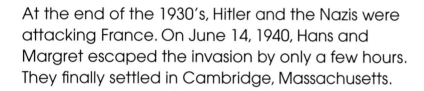

Did You Know..?

- **Hans built two Bicycles for them to use in their escape from the Nazis.**

- **Hans had the ideas and the illustrations, and Margret wrote the stories.**

- **The Boston Children's Hospital asked them to write a story about George in the hospital.**

Activity One

Which word **rhymes** **with the word from the story?**

1.	mat	name	what	came	hat
2.	it	ship	mice	trip	ice
3.	tire	fire	wire	weird	when
4.	stop	pop	pot	top	on
5.	we	fell	tree	sea	free

Activity Two

Read the word. **Say** the word. Which kind of **vowel sound** does each word have? Circle your answers.

1. happy

   long a
   short a
   silent a

2. paid

   silent a
   short a
   long a

3. water

   long a
   short a
   silent a

4. bed

   short e
   long e
   silent e

5. easy

   silent e
   long e
   short e

6. came

   long a
   silent a
   short a

Curious George CC2100

Activity Three

Fill in the blanks with the following (digraphs forming) words from the story.

wh   **th**   **sh**

1. __ __ e y

2. __ __ a t

3. __ __ e m

4. __ __ i p

5. __ __ i n

6. __ __ i s k

7. __ __ o r e

8. __ __ r e e

9. __ __ o w e d

Activity Four

Underline the words that have a **short e** sound.

Circle the words that have a **long e** sound.

Examples: <u>head</u>   (bee)

1. bed

2. he

3. fell

4. easy

5. deck

6. tree

7. very

8. sea

9. then

10. three

11. belt

12. be

13. street

14. reach

15. held

Activity Five

Write a word from the story that has double consonants or double vowels.

1. y e ____ o w   **2.** h ____ k   **3.** z ____

4. g u ____ s   **5.** f ____ l   **6.** t h r ____

7. s t o ____ e d   **8.** p o ____ e d   **9.** l i ____ l e

10. h a ____ y   **11.** s t r u ____ l i n g   **12.** g ____ d

Activity Six

Fill in the chart with the words from the list.

big	higher	instead	mixed	tired
fight	l	light	ship	wind
fire	in	like	signal	wire

Short i (is)

_____
_____
_____
_____
_____
_____

Long i (ice)

_____
_____
_____
_____
_____
_____

Activity Seven

Change the first letter or last letter to make a (new) word.

Examples:

yet ⇨ (m) e t   hat ⇨ h a (d)

1. map ⇨ ◯ a p
2. bed ⇨ ◯ e d
3. fell ⇨ ◯ e l l
4. hat ⇨ ◯ a t
5. light ⇨ ◯ i g h t
6. paid ⇨ p a i ◯
7. he ⇨ ◯ e
8. wall ⇨ ◯ a l l

Activity Eight

Fill in the blank with the proper word from the story.

1. The _____ guests/gusts of wind rocked the boat.

2. George's major _____ faught/fault was that he was curious.

3. Once on the deck George saw some _____ see/sea gulls.

4. The man picked the monkey up _____ quietly/quickly and popped him into the bag.

5. The firemen looked for the _____ sing/signal on the map that _____ snowed/showed where the call came from.

Activity Nine

Find the words in the story. Fill in the blanks with the letters from the list. The first one has been done for you.

ea	**ou**	**oo**	**oa**	**au**

1. r _e_ _a_ l

2. b ___ ___ r d

3. ___ ___ s y

4. n ___ ___ghty

5. m ___ ___ l

6. s t ___ ___ l

7. b ___ ___ t

8. t r ___ ___ ble

9. f ___ ___ nd

Activity Ten

 the word. the word. How many different does the word have?

Example:
    made ⇨ ①

1. firemen ⇨ ◯

2. forget ⇨ ◯

3. lightning ⇨ ◯

4. watchman ⇨ ◯

5. department ⇨ ◯

6. telephone ⇨ ◯

7. balloon ⇨ ◯

8. altogether ⇨ ◯

9. curious ⇨ ◯

10. fascinated ⇨ ◯

Activity Eleven

1. **Draw** a line from the beginning of the word to the end of the word. **Say** the word. **Write** the word on the line. The first one has been done for you.

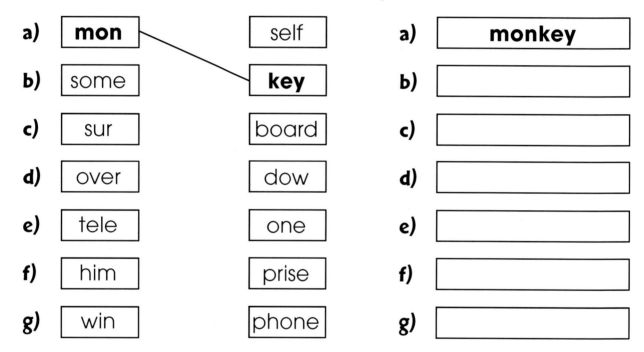

a)	mon	self	a)	monkey	
b)	some	key	b)		
c)	sur	board	c)		
d)	over	dow	d)		
e)	tele	one	e)		
f)	him	prise	f)		
g)	win	phone	g)		

2. Choose **two** words from the list above. Use each word in a full sentence. Remember to begin your sentence with a **capital letter** and end it with a **period.**

Sentence One

_____

Sentence Two

_____

NAME: _____

Activity One

Write the words in ABC order.

1.	wire	fault	paid	shore	bed	tree

_____

2.	wind	mixed	light	signal	gulls	wall

_____

3.	instead	like	easy	nice	promise	did

_____

Activity Two

1. **Yellow is an adjective found in the story. Find ten more adjectives in the book. Write them in a list. Be sure to number your list!**

Adjectives

_____   _____

_____   _____

_____   _____

_____   _____

2. **Write a full sentence using as many adjectives from your list as possible.**

_____

 Word Study

Activity Three

Write a word from the story that means the **opposite of** each of these words.

1. tiny [   ]   2. easy [   ]

3. night [   ]   4. unsafe [   ]

5. slowly [   ]   6. many [   ]

7. slow [   ]   8. brother [   ]

Activity Four

Write the words in proper sentence order.

1. bed   fell   He   and   into   crawled asleep

_____

2. didn't What   do?   George   to   know   how

_____

3. a   little   thought. nice   "What   monkey," he

_____

NAME: _____

Word Study

Activity Five

A full sentence is a complete thought. Are these sentences full sentences? Circle Yes or No.

1. George was caught in the bag.   Yes   No

2. What a nice place for George to live!   Yes   No

3. Ding-a-ling-a-ling.   Yes   No

4. On to the hook-and-ladders   Yes   No

5. Everyone out of the way!   Yes   No

6. Only a naughty little monkey.   Yes   No

Activity Six

Add the ending to the root word to make a new word.
Example:

slow + ly   = | slowly |

1. quick + ly   = [   ]   2. final + ly   = [   ]

3. struggle + ing = [   ]   4. blow + ing = [   ]

5. quiet + ly   = [   ]   6. sail + ing   = [   ]

7. row + ing   = [   ]   8. go + ing   = [   ]

© CLASSROOM COMPLETE PRESS   **Curious George CC2100**

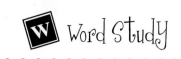 **Word Study**

Activity Seven

Fill in each blank with the correct verb from the story.

1. He _____ how the gulls could fly.

2. He _____ into bed and fell _____
    at once.

3. Then the man _____ away.

4. You _____ the Fire Department.

Activity Eight

Fill in each blank with the correct adjective from the story.

1. He had on a _____, _____, _____ hat.

2. He felt he must have a _____, _____
    balloon.

3. What a _____ place for George to live.

4. George said good-bye to the _____sailors.

Activity Nine

1. **At the end of each sentence put a period (.), question mark (?) or exclamation mark (!).**

    a) Man overboard _____

    b) Where is George _____

    c) No fire _____

    d) The firemen rushed into the building _____

    e) He was free _____

    f) Finally it stopped blowing altogether _____

2. **Make up** **three** **sentences of your own. Write one that ends with a** **period.** **Write a second that ends with an** **exclamation mark.** **Make the last one a question that ends with a** **question mark.**

    Sentence - ends with a period (.)

    _____

    Sentence - ends with an exclamation mark (!)

    _____

    Question - ends with a question mark (?)

    _____

NAME: _____

Activity Ten

1. A **noun** is a person, place or thing. Choose **four** nouns from the story. **Write** them on the lines. **Draw** a picture to show what the word means.

    a) _____

    b) _____

    c) _____

    d) _____

2. Choose **one** noun from Question 1 above. Use it in your own sentence. Write your sentence on the lines. Remember to begin your sentence with a **capital letter** and end it with a **period.**

    _____

    _____

Activity One

Put a check mark (✓) next to the answer that is correct.

1. **George is a happy monkey who lived where?**
   - ○ **A** He lived in Austria.
   - ○ **B** He lived in Australia.
   - ○ **C** He lived in Africa.

2. **What did the man with the large yellow hat want with a monkey?**
   - ○ **A** He wanted to bring George fishing.
   - ○ **B** He wanted to bring George to the Zoo.
   - ○ **C** He wanted to sell George.

3. **What did George want to learn how to do?**
   - ○ **A** He wanted to fly like the gulls.
   - ○ **B** He wanted to sail like the sailors.
   - ○ **C** He wanted to hunt like the hunters.

4. **How did the sailors save George?**
   - ○ **A** They jumped in the water and got him.
   - ○ **B** The threw him a rope.
   - ○ **C** The threw him a lifebelt.

5. **Where was George's new and nice place to live?**
   - ○ **A** The Insectarium.
   - ○ **B** The City Gardens.
   - ○ **C** The Zoo.

NAME: _____

Activity Two

Circle the **T** if the sentence is true.
Circle **F** if it is false (not true).

T F **1.** George was caught in the United States.

T F **2.** They saw him struggling in the water, and almost all tired out.

T F **3.** George called 9-1-1.

T F **4.** The man telephoned the Zoo.

T F **5.** George wanted to fly like the robins.

T F **6.** The Firemen jumped onto the fire engine and onto the hook-and-ladders.

T F **7.** George was in a lightning storm.

T F **8.** They took George and shut him in the prison.

T F **9.** The man brought George back to Africa.

T F **10.** George flew in the wind while holding the balloons.

 Comprehension

Activity Three

Number the events from ❶ to ❿ in the order they happened in the story.

◯   George saw the man call the Zoo. He wanted to try and ended up calling the Fire Department.

◯   George walked along the telephone lines after he escaped from prison.

◯   George wanted to fly like the sea gulls but that only got him in the water.

◯   George was curious and wanted to put on the large yellow straw hat.

◯   Once at the man's house, George ate and slept.

◯   The man paid for George's balloons.

◯   The monkey left Africa on a ship.

◯   The monkey wanted the bright red balloon but he took the whole bunch.

◯   The Zoo was a nice place to live.

◯   They took him away and they shut him in the prison.

NAME: _____

Activity Four

Who said each statement? Use the characters in the list.

The man   The firemen   The sailors   George

1 "What a nice little monkey."

2 "Hello! Hello!"

3 "Now run along, play but don't get into trouble."

4 "Oh, catch him, catch him."

5 "GEORGE!"

6 "Where is George?"

7 "You fooled the Fire Department."

8 "Man overboard!"

9 "We will have to shut you up where you can't do any more harm."

10 "I would like to take him home with me."

NAME: _____

Activity Five

Match the question with the correct answer.

1	Who flew over the traffic light?	The sea gulls.	A
2	Who did the little girl buy a balloon for?	The monkey.	B
3	Who was too big and heavy?	The thin and the fat firemen.	C
4	Who did the man give money to?	George.	D
5	Who dialed 1-2-3-4-5-6-7 ?	The sailors.	E
6	Who threw George a lifebelt?	Her brother.	F
7	Who flew over the ship?	The balloon man.	G
8	Who did George say good-bye to?	The watchman.	H
9	Who made the bed tip over?	The watchman.	I
10	Who brought George to the prison?	The sailors.	J

NAME: _____

Activity Six

1 List <u>five</u> words that describe George. List <u>five</u> words that describe the man that caught George. Remember to number your lists!

George	The man
_____	_____
_____	_____
_____	_____
_____	_____
_____	_____

2 (Circle) the words that tell what the firemen and sailors looked like.

thin	worried	fat	men
strong	happy	women	mad

3 <u>Underline</u> the words that tell where George went in the story.

In a fire	In a prison	In traffic	On wires
In a boat	On a ship	In a home	In a bed

28

Curious George CC2100

Draw a picture of your new pet.

The man in the yellow hat went to Africa and he came back with a monkey. Do you think this is how most people get new pets? If you were to get a new pet, how would you go about it? Where would you go to find it?

Page One

NAME: _____

Draw a picture of a monkey (or another wild animal) in a zoo.

The man in the yellow hat brought a wild monkey from Africa to the United States and put him in a Zoo. Do you **agree** or **disagree** with taking animals from their **natural habitats** and putting them in a zoo to be watched all day long? How could this benefit the animal? How could it benefit people?

Page Two

NAME: _____

Draw a picture of Curious George in one of his *predicaments.*

Page Three

Curious George is extremely curious. Why do you think he's so curious? Do you think he is showing good behavior? Why or why not?

NAME: _____

Draw a picture of you interviewing the man in the large yellow straw hat.

Page Four

Imagine you are a newspaper reporter. You are going to schedule an interview with the man in the large yellow straw hat. What questions will you ask this man? Write down five questions you definitely want to ask him.

Curious George CC2100

NAME: _____

Draw a picture of a no smoking sign.

Page Five

At the man's home, George eats, smokes and then sleeps. Smoking is very dangerous to one's health. Why do you think the author wrote about the monkey smoking the pipe? Do you think the intention was to get attention? Was it to make a statement? Do you agree with this passage? Why or why not?

33

NAME: _____

Draw a picture of a Zoo.

Have you ever visited a zoo, or another place where wild animals are kept in captivity? If so, what did you like about the zoo? What didn't you like about the zoo? Explain your answers.

Page Six

Activity One

Curious George is very curious. **Curious** is a **describing word** that tells us about George. What other describing words could you use for George?

Write an **acrostic poem** about Curious George. Each line of your poem will begin with a letter in his name. For your poem, choose words that you think describe him best. Try to use different words, especially for letters that are repeated.

C _____

U _____

R _____

I _____

O _____

U _____

S _____

G _____

E _____

O _____

R _____

G _____

E _____

Activity Two

Curious George is so curious that he often gets himself into trouble. Help him keep his promise to the man in the yellow hat, and stay safe and out of trouble. Write a list of Safety Rules for George to follow.

Stay Safe! Rules for Monkeys

Things Monkeys May Do

1 _____

2 _____

3 _____

4 _____

Stay Safe!

Things Monkeys Are NOT to Do

1 _____

2 _____

3 _____

4 _____

Activity Three

In this story, when George smoked the pipe, did you think to yourself, "**George, smoking is dangerous for your health**"?

Posters and advertising can show us that smoking is an unhealthy thing to do. Make a **poster** and a **slogan** to encourage people not to smoke. Be sure to list good reasons why people shouldn't smoke.

Activity Four

Your mind is made up – you would like a new pet. You are sure that having a pet is a good idea, and you see no problems in having one. Your parents, on the other hand, are not so sure.

Decide what kind of pet you would like. **Brainstorm** a list of pros and cons to having this pet. The pros are good reasons to have the pet. The cons are things that may be problems or difficulties.

I would like a _____ **for a pet.**

PROS (Good Reasons)	CONS (Problems or Difficulties)

Read your list of pros and cons. Do you think it is still a good idea to have this pet? If so, present your findings to your parents. Good Luck!

Activity Five

Your younger siblings love Curious George. They want you to help them make a Curious George craft. What craft will you show them how to make? Be sure that your craft has something important to do with the story. What materials will you need? What steps are needed to make it? Write out the instructions below.

How to Make a _____
Title of craft

You will need:

_____

_____

_____

_____

Drawing of craft

Steps:

_____

_____

_____

_____

_____

Activity Six

At the end of the story George has a nice place to live at the Zoo. But even at the Zoo, he is still very curious! Think of a **new adventure** that George has at the Zoo. Write about his adventure. Tell **all about** the trouble he gets into now.

NAME: _____

Crossword

Read the clues below. Write the answer where you find the correct number. Be careful! Some words go down. Some words go across.

Across

1. Always keep a _____ you make.

5. Lots of monkeys live in _____.

8. She climbed the _____ to get on the roof.

9. I have one sister and one _____ .

12. Yellow fruit with a peel

13. Wait for the green _____ to cross the road.

Down

2. Another word for boat

3. It's not his _____ because he didn't do it.

4. To watch over something to keep it safe

6. Someone you play with

7. George was a _____ monkey.

10. Cars driving on the road are called _____ .

11. Do not hurt or _____ the animals.

Curious George CC2100

Word Search

Find the words in the Word Search puzzle. Circle them.

caught	department	fascinated	gulls
lifebelt	lightning	naughty	overboard
prison	sailors	struggling	surprised

D	E	T	A	N	I	C	S	A	F
E	E	P	R	I	S	O	N	N	F
S	J	P	C	A	U	G	H	T	F
I	D	R	A	O	B	R	E	V	O
R	Y	S	S	R	O	L	I	A	S
P	L	I	G	H	T	N	I	N	G
R	S	L	L	U	G	M	M	E	Q
U	J	L	I	F	E	B	E	L	T
S	T	R	U	G	G	L	I	N	G
Y	T	H	G	U	A	N	T	F	T

Vocabulary Cards

fault	**curious**
caught	**stool**
promise	**gulls**
sailors	**struggling**
overboard	**shore**

A B C Vocabulary

NAME: _____

Vocabulary Cards

fascinated	naughty
department	harm
lightning	gust
whisk	prison
watchman	signal

Vocabulary Cards

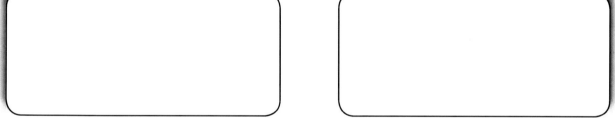

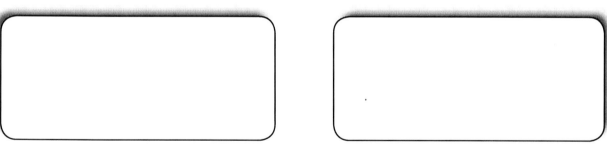

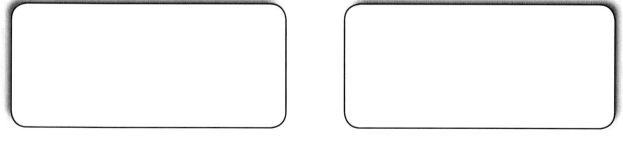

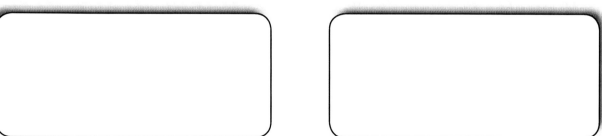

Comprehension Quiz

1.　Fill in the blanks.

a)　The man wore a large yellow straw _____.

b)　He caught the monkey and popped him in a _____.

c)　The man wanted to bring him to a _____.

d)　On the ship, George _____ that he wouldn't get into trouble.

e)　It is easy for little monkeys to _____.

2.　Match the character with the item.

a) firemen	large yellow straw hat
b) brother	ship
c) gulls	bright red balloon
d) sailors	the prison
e) the little girl	sister
f) the man	hook-and-ladder
g) watchman	the sea

SUBTOTAL:　/12

Comprehension Quiz

Answer the questions in full sentences.

3. Why did the man pay the balloon man?

   _____

   _____ ②

4. How did George feel when he was sailing high over the houses?

   _____

   _____ ②

5. How did George act in the water?

   _____

   _____ ②

6. Why did they put George in prison?

   _____

   _____ ②

7. Who did George call?

   _____

   _____ ②

8. What did they say about the call?

   _____

   _____ ②

9. What did the firemen think of George?

   _____

   _____ ②

10. Where does George end up at last?

    _____

    _____ ②

SUBTOTAL: /16

1.

1. hat
2. ship, trip
3. fire, wire
4. pop, top
5. tree, sea, free

2.

1. short a   2. long a   3. short a
4. short e   5. long e   6. long a

3.

1. they   2. what /that   3. them
4. ship   5. thin   6. whisk
7. shore   8. three   9. showed

4.

1. short   2. long   3. short
4. long   5. short   6. long
7. short   8. long   9. short
10. long   11. short   12. long
13. long   14. long   15. short

5.

1. yellow   2. hook   3. zoo
4. gulls   5. feel   6. three
7. stopped   8. popped   9. little
10. happy   11. struggling   12. good

6.

Short i:	Long i:
big	higher
instead	tired
mixed	fight
ship	I
wind	light
in	fire
signal	like
	wire

7.

Possible answers

1. nap   2. red
3. well   4. sat
5. right   6. pail
7. me   8. tall

8.

1. gusts
2. fault
3. sea
4. quickly
5. signal, showed

9.

1. real   2. board   3. easy
4. naughty   5. meal   6. stool
7. boat   8. trouble   9. found

10.

1. ③   2. ②
3. ②   4. ②
5. ③   6. ③
7. ②   8. ④
9. ③   10. ④

11 12 13 14 15

7.
1. wondered
2. crawled, asleep
3. got
4. fooled

8.
1. large, yellow, straw
2. bright, red
3. nice
4. kind

5.
1. yes
2. yes
3. no
4. no
5. yes
6. no

6.
1. quickly
2. finally
3. struggling
4. blowing
5. quietly
6. sailing
7. rowing
8. going

3.
Possible answers:

1. big
2. hard
3. day
4. safe
5. quickly
6. few
7. fast
8. sister

4.
1. He crawled into bed and fell asleep.
2. What didn't George know how to do?
3. "What a nice little monkey," he thought.

1.
1.
bed, fault, paid, shore, tree, wire

2.
gulls, light, mixed, signal, wall, wind

3.
did, easy, instead, like, nice, promise

2.
1. Possible answers:

large, straw, thin, big, red, bright, sea, nice, little, good, real, heavy

2. Answers will vary

11.
1.
b) someone
c) surprise
d) overboard
e) telephone
f) himself
g) window

2. Answers will vary

EZ✓

3. ⑤ ⑦ ③ ① ④ ⑨ ② ⑧ ⑩ ⑥

25

2.
1. **F**
2. **T**
3. **F**
4. **T**
5. **F**
6. **T**
7. **F**
8. **T**
9. **F**
10. **T**

24

1.
1. C
2. B
3. B
4. C
5. C

23

10. Answers will vary

22

9.
1.
a) !
b) ?
c) :
d) .
e) :
f) .

2. Answers will vary

21

Across:

1. promise
5. Africa
8. ladder
9. brother
12. bananas
13. signal

Down:

2. ship
3. fault
4. guard
6. friend
7. curious
10. traffic
11. harm

(29) (30) (31) (32) (33) (34)

Reading Response
All answers will vary

(35) (36) (37) (38) (39) (40)

Writing Tasks
All answers will vary

(41)

6.

1. Answers will vary

2.
   thin
   worried,
   fat,
   men,
   strong,
   happy,
   mad

3.
   in a boat,
   in a prison,
   on a ship,
   in traffic,
   in a home,
   on wires,
   in a bed

(28)

5.

1. (B) or (D)
2. (F)
3. (H)
4. (G)
5. (B) or (D)
6. (E) or (J)
7. (A)
8. (E) or (J)
9. (I)
10. (C)

(27)

4.

1. the sailors
2. the firemen
3. the man
4. the firemen
5. the sailors
6. the sailors
7. the firemen
8. the sailors
9. the firemen
10. the man

(26)

3. George took the bunch of balloons

4. Frightened

5. Struggling

6. So that he could not harm anyone

7. Fire Department

8. They thought the call was for a real fire.

9. They were mad at George for calling them for nothing.

10. A nice place to live at the Zoo

1.

a) hat

b) bag

c) Zoo

d) promised

e) forget

2.

a) hook-and-ladder

b) sister

c) the sea

d) ship

e) bright red balloon

f) large yellow straw hat

g) the prison

Word Search Answers

1.
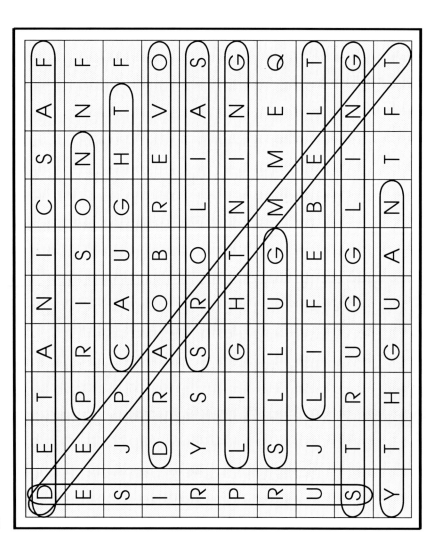

2. fast, burn, paper, trail, huge, door

Curious George CC2100

My Feelings

• • • • • • • • • • • • • •

How did you feel when you read the story, Curious George? Think about the different things that happened to George and the trouble he got into. Write down these events from the story. Then tell how you felt as you read about each event.

Example:
• **When I read about** the man catching George in the bag...

• **I felt** sad for George, happy for the man

EVENT When I read about ...	FEELINGS I felt ...

Sum It up!

In this story Curious George has many adventures.
He gets into one *predicament* after another. Choose one of the
problems that he gets into. Then answer the questions to *sum up* the
event (tell how the event happened).

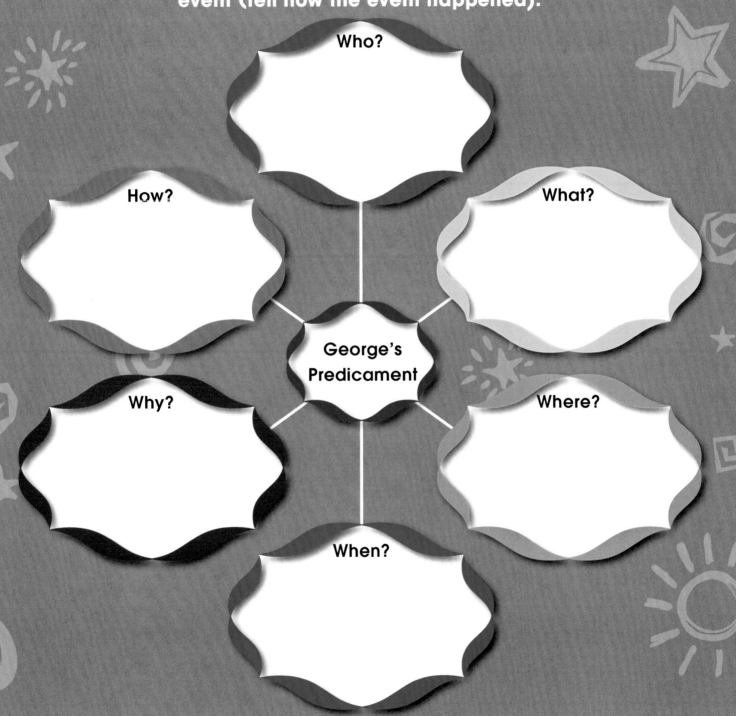

Who?

How?

What?

George's Predicament

Why?

Where?

When?

Curious George CC2100

Mixed Up = Pu Dexim

CHOOSE FIFTEEN INTERESTING WORDS FROM THE STORY.
WRITE THEM ON A SEPARATE SHEET OF PAPER. THEN REWRITE THE WORDS
IN A LIST BELOW SO THAT THEY ARE ALL MIXED UP.

Switch lists with a partner. Try to unscramble your partner's words.
Your partner is to unscramble your words. The first one is done for you. Have fun!

Mixed Up Words

1. gorege
2.
3.
4.
5.
6.
7.
8.
9.
10.
11.
12.
13.
14.
15.

Unscrambled Words

1. George
2.
3.
4.
5.
6.
7.
8.
9.
10.
11.
12.
13.
14.
15.

- **RSL.K.1** With prompting and support, ask and answer questions about key details in a text.
- **RSL.K.2** With prompting and support, retell familiar stories, including key details.
- **RSL.K.3** With prompting and support, identify characters, settings, and major events in a story.
- **RSL.K.4** Ask and answer questions about unknown words in a text.
- **RSL.K.5** Recognize common types of texts.
- **RSL.K.6** With prompting and support, name the author and illustrator of a story and define the role of each in telling the story.
- **RSL.K.7** With prompting and support, describe the relationship between illustrations and the story in which they appear.
- **RSL.K.9** With prompting and support, compare and contrast the adventures and experiences of characters in familiar stories.
- **RSL.K.10** Actively engage in group reading activities with purpose and understanding.
- **RSL.1.1** Ask and answer questions about key details in a text.
- **RSL.1.2** Retell stories, including key details, and demonstrate understanding of their central message or lesson.
- **RSL.1.3** Describe characters, settings, and major events in a story, using key details.
- **RSL.1.4** Identify words and phrases in stories or poems that suggest feelings or appeal to the senses.
- **RSL.1.5** Explain major differences between books that tell stories and books that give information, drawing on a wide reading of a range of text types.
- **RSL.1.6** Identify who is telling the story at various points in a text.
- **RSL.1.7** Use illustrations and details in a story to describe its characters, setting, or events.
- **RSL.1.9** Compare and contrast the adventures and experiences of characters in stories.
- **RSL.1.10** With prompting and support, read prose and poetry of appropriate complexity for grade 1.
- **RSL.2.1** Ask and answer such questions as *who*, *what*, *where*, *when*, *why*, and *how* to demonstrate understanding of key details in a text.
- **RSL.2.2** Recount stories, including fables and folktales from diverse cultures, and determine their central message, lesson, or moral.
- **RSL.2.3** Describe how characters in a story respond to major events and challenges.
- **RSL.2.4** Describe how words and phrases supply rhythm and meaning in a story, poem, or song.
- **RSL.2.5** Describe the overall structure of a story, including describing how the beginning introduces the story and the ending concludes the action.
- **RSL.2.6** Acknowledge differences in the points of view of characters, including by speaking in a different voice for each character when reading dialogue aloud.
- **RSL.2.7** Use information gained from the illustrations and words in a print or digital text to demonstrate understanding of its characters, setting, or plot.
- **RSL.2.9** Compare and contrast two or more versions of the same story by different authors or from different cultures.
- **RSL.2.10** By the end of the year read and comprehend literature, including stories and poetry, in the grades 2–3 text complexity band proficiently, with scaffolding as needed at the high end of the range.
- **RSFS.1.1** Read with sufficient accuracy and fluency to support comprehension. **A)** Read grade-level text with purpose and understanding. **B)** Read grade-level prose and poetry orally with accuracy, appropriate rate, and expression on successive readings. **C)** Use context to confirm or self-correct word recognition and understanding, rereading as necessary.
- **RSFS.1.1** Demonstrate understanding of the organization and basic features of print. **A)** Recognize the distinguishing features of a sentence.
- **RSFS.1.2** Demonstrate understanding of spoken words, syllables, and sounds. **A)** Distinguish long from short vowel sounds in spoken single-syllable words. b. Orally produce single-syllable words by blending sounds, including consonant blends. c. Isolate and pronounce initial, medial vowel, and final sounds in spoken single-syllable words. d. Segment spoken single-syllable words into their complete sequence of individual sounds.
- **RSFS.1.3** Know and apply grade-level phonics and word analysis skills in decoding words. a. Know the spelling-sound correspondences for common consonant digraphs. **B)** Decode regularly spelled one-syllable words. **C)** Know final -e and common vowel team conventions for representing long vowel sounds. **D)** Use knowledge that every syllable must have a vowel sound to determine the number of syllables in a printed word. **E)** Decode two-syllable words following basic patterns by breaking the words into syllables. f. Read words with inflectional endings. **G)** Recognize and read grade-appropriate irregularly spelled words.
- **RSFS.1.4** Read with sufficient accuracy and fluency to support comprehension. **A)** Read grade-level text with purpose and understanding. **B)** Read grade-level text orally with accuracy, appropriate rate, and expression on successive readings. **C)** Use context to confirm or self-correct word recognition and understanding, rereading as necessary.
- **RSFS.2.3** Know and apply grade-level phonics and word analysis skills in decoding words. **A)** Distinguish long and short vowels when reading regularly spelled one-syllable words. **B)** Know spelling-sound correspondences for additional common vowel teams. **C)** Decode regularly spelled two-syllable words with long vowels. **D)** Decode words with common prefixes and suffixes. **E)** Identify words with inconsistent but common spelling-sound correspondences. **F)** Recognize and read grade-appropriate irregularly spelled words.
- **RSFS.2.4** Read with sufficient accuracy and fluency to support comprehension. **A)** Read grade-level text with purpose and understanding. **B)** Read grade-level text orally with accuracy, appropriate rate, and expression on successive readings. **C)** Use context to confirm or self-correct word recognition and understanding, rereading as necessary.
- **WS.1.1** Write opinion pieces in which they introduce the topic or name the book they are writing about, state an opinion, supply a reason for the opinion, and provide some sense of closure.
- **WS.1.2** Write informative/explanatory texts in which they name a topic, supply some facts about the topic, and provide some sense of closure.
- **WS.1.3** Write narratives in which they recount two or more appropriately sequenced events, include some details regarding what happened, use temporal words to signal event order, and provide some sense of closure.
- **WS.1.5** With guidance and support from adults, focus on a topic, respond to questions and suggestions from peers, and add details to strengthen writing as needed.
- **WS.1.8** With guidance and support from adults, recall information from experiences or gather information from provided sources to answer a question.
- **WS.2.1** Write opinion pieces in which they introduce the topic or book they are writing about, state an opinion, supply reasons that support the opinion, use linking words to connect opinion and reasons, and provide a concluding statement or section.
- **WS.2.2** Write informative/explanatory texts in which they introduce a topic, use facts and definitions to develop points, and provide a concluding statement or section.
- **WS.2.3** Write narratives in which they recount a well elaborated event or short sequence of events, include details to describe actions, thoughts, and feelings, use temporal words to signal event order, and provide a sense of closure.
- **WS.2.8** Recall information from experiences or gather information from provided sources to answer a question.

Publication Listing

Ask Your Dealer About Our Complete Line

VISIT:
www.CLASSROOM COMPLETE PRESS.com

To view sample pages from each book

COMMON CORE

LITERATURE KITS™ - Books

ITEM #	TITLE
	GRADES 1-2
CC2100	Curious George (H. A. Rey)
CC2101	Paper Bag Princess (Robert N. Munsch)
CC2102	Stone Soup (Marcia Brown)
CC2103	The Very Hungry Caterpillar (Eric Carle)
CC2104	Where the Wild Things Are (Maurice Sendak)
	GRADES 3-4
CC2300	Babe: The Gallant Pig (Dick King-Smith)
CC2301	Because of Winn-Dixie (Kate DiCamillo)
CC2302	The Tale of Despereaux (Kate DiCamillo)
CC2303	James and the Giant Peach (Roald Dahl)
CC2304	Ramona Quimby, Age 8 (Beverly Cleary)
CC2305	The Mouse and the Motorcycle (Beverly Cleary)
CC2306	Charlotte's Web (E.B. White)
CC2307	Owls in the Family (Farley Mowat)
CC2308	Sarah, Plain and Tall (Patricia MacLachlan)
CC2309	Matilda (Roald Dahl)
CC2310	Charlie & The Chocolate Factory (Roald Dahl)
CC2311	Frindle (Andrew Clements)
CC2312	M.C. Higgins, the Great (Virginia Hamilton)
CC2313	The Family Under The Bridge (N.S. Carlson)
CC2314	The Hundred Penny Box (Sharon Mathis)
CC2315	Cricket in Times Square (George Selden)
	GRADES 5-6
CC2500	Black Beauty (Anna Sewell)
CC2501	Bridge to Terabithia (Katherine Paterson)
CC2502	Bud, Not Buddy (Christopher Paul Curtis)
CC2503	The Egypt Game (Zilpha Keatley Snyder)
CC2504	The Great Gilly Hopkins (Katherine Paterson)
CC2505	Holes (Louis Sachar)
CC2506	Number the Stars (Lois Lowry)
CC2507	The Sign of the Beaver (E.G. Speare)
CC2508	The Whipping Boy (Sid Fleischman)
CC2509	Island of the Blue Dolphins (Scott O'Dell)
CC2510	Underground to Canada (Barbara Smucker)
CC2511	Loser (Jerry Spinelli)
CC2512	The Higher Power of Lucky (Susan Patron)
CC2513	Kira-Kira (Cynthia Kadohata)
CC2514	Dear Mr. Henshaw (Beverly Cleary)
CC2515	The Summer of the Swans (Betsy Byars)
CC2516	Shiloh (Phyllis Reynolds Naylor)
CC2517	A Single Shard (Linda Sue Park)
CC2518	Hoot (Carl Hiaasen)
CC2519	Hatchet (Gary Paulsen)
CC2520	The Giver (Lois Lowry)
CC2521	The Graveyard Book (Neil Gaiman)
CC2522	The View From Saturday (E.L Konigsburg)
CC2523	Hattie Big Sky (Kirby Larson)
CC2524	When You Reach Me (Rebecca Stead)
CC2525	Criss Cross (Lynne Rae Perkins)
CC2526	A Year Down Yonder (Richard Peak)
	GRADES 7-8
CC2700	Cheaper by the Dozen (Frank B. Gilbreth)
CC2701	The Miracle Worker (William Gibson)
CC2702	The Red Pony (John Steinbeck)
CC2703	Treasure Island (Robert Louis Stevenson)
CC2704	Romeo & Juliet (William Shakespeare)
CC2705	Crispin: The Cross of Lead (Avi)

LITERATURE KITS™ - Books

ITEM #	TITLE
	GRADES 9-12
CC2001	To Kill A Mockingbird (Harper Lee)
CC2002	Angela's Ashes (Frank McCourt)
CC2003	The Grapes of Wrath (John Steinbeck)
CC2004	The Good Earth (Pearl S. Buck)
CC2005	The Road (Cormac McCarthy)
CC2006	The Old Man and the Sea (Ernest Hemingway)
CC2007	Lord of the Flies (William Golding)
CC2008	The Color Purple (Alice Walker)
CC2009	The Outsiders (S.E. Hinton)
CC2010	Hamlet (William Shakespeare)

LANGUAGE ARTS - Software

ITEM #	TITLE
	WORD FAMILIES SERIES
CC7112	Word Families - Short Vowels Grades PK-2
CC7113	Word Families - Long Vowels Grades PK-2
CC7114	Word Families - Vowels Big Box Grades PK-2
	SIGHT & PICTURE WORDS SERIES
CC7100	High Frequency Sight Words Grades PK-2
CC7101	High Frequency Picture Words Grades PK-2
CC7102	Sight & Picture Words Big Box Grades PK-2
	WRITING SKILLS SERIES
CC7104	How to Write a Paragraph Grades 5-8
CC7105	How to Write a Book Report Grades 5-8
CC7106	How to Write an Essay Grades 5-8
CC7107	Master Writing Big Box Grades 5-8
	READING SKILLS SERIES
CC7108	Reading Comprehension Grades 3-8
CC7109	Literary Devices Grades 3-8
CC7110	Critical Thinking Grades 3-8
CC7111	Master Reading Big Box Grades 3-8

LANGUAGE ARTS - Books

ITEM #	TITLE
	WORD FAMILIES SERIES
CC1110	Word Families - Short Vowels Grades PK-1
CC1111	Word Families - Long Vowels Grades PK-1
CC1112	Word Families - Vowels Big Book Grades K-1
	SIGHT & PICTURE WORDS SERIES
CC1113	High Frequency Sight Words Grades PK-1
CC1114	High Frequency Picture Words Grades PK-1
CC1115	Sight & Picture Words Big Book Grades PK-1
	WRITING SKILLS SERIES
CC1100	How to Write a Paragraph Grades 5-8
CC1101	How to Write a Book Report Grades 5-8
CC1102	How to Write an Essay Grades 5-8
CC1103	Master Writing Big Book Grades 5-8
	READING SKILLS SERIES
CC7108	Reading Comprehension Grades 5-8
CC7109	Literary Devices Grades 5-8
CC7110	Critical Thinking Grades 5-8
CC7111	Master Reading Big Book Grades 5-8
	READING RESPONSE FORMS SERIES
CC1106	Reading Response Forms: Grades 1-2
CC1107	Reading Response Forms: Grades 3-4
CC1108	Reading Response Forms: Grades 5-6
CC1109	Reading Response Forms Big Book: Grades 1-6

MATHEMATICS - Software

ITEM #	TITLE
	PRINCIPLES & STANDARDS OF MATH SERIES
CC7315	Grades PK-2 Five Strands of Math Big Box
CC7316	Grades 3-5 Five Strands of Math Big Box
CC7317	Grades 6-8 Five Strands of Math Big Box

MATHEMATICS - Books

ITEM #	TITLE
	PRINCIPLES & STANDARDS OF MATH SERIES
CC3100	Grades PK-2 Number & Operations Task Sheets
CC3101	Grades PK-2 Algebra Task Sheets
CC3102	Grades PK-2 Geometry Task Sheets
CC3103	Grades PK-2 Measurement Task Sheets
CC3104	Grades PK-2 Data Analysis & Probability Task Sheets
CC3105	Grades PK-2 Five Strands of Math Big Book Task Sheets
CC3106	Grades 3-5 Number & Operations Task Sheets
CC3107	Grades 3-5 Algebra Task Sheets
CC3108	Grades 3-5 Geometry Task Sheets
CC3109	Grades 3-5 Measurement Task Sheets
CC3110	Grades 3-5 Data Analysis & Probability Task Sheets
CC3111	Grades 3-5 Five Strands of Math Big Book Task Sheets
CC3112	Grades 6-8 Number & Operations Task Sheets
CC3113	Grades 6-8 Algebra Task Sheets
CC3114	Grades 6-8 Geometry Task Sheets
CC3115	Grades 6-8 Measurement Task Sheets
CC3116	Grades 6-8 Data Analysis & Probability Task Sheets
CC3117	Grades 6-8 Five Strands of Math Big Book Task Sheets
	PRINCIPLES & STANDARDS OF MATH SERIES
CC3200	Grades PK-2 Number & Operations Drill Sheets
CC3201	Grades PK-2 Algebra Drill Sheets
CC3202	Grades PK-2 Geometry Drill Sheets
CC3203	Grades PK-2 Measurement Drill Sheets
CC3204	Grades PK-2 Data Analysis & Probability Drill Sheets
CC3205	Grades PK-2 Five Strands of Math Big Book Drill Sheets
CC3206	Grades 3-5 Number & Operations Drill Sheets
CC3207	Grades 3-5 Algebra Drill Sheets
CC3208	Grades 3-5 Geometry Drill Sheets
CC3209	Grades 3-5 Measurement Drill Sheets
CC3210	Grades 3-5 Data Analysis & Probability Drill Sheets
CC3211	Grades 3-5 Five Strands of Math Big Book Drill Sheets
CC3212	Grades 6-8 Number & Operations Drill Sheets
CC3213	Grades 6-8 Algebra Drill Sheets
CC3214	Grades 6-8 Geometry Drill Sheets
CC3215	Grades 6-8 Measurement Drill Sheets
CC3216	Grades 6-8 Data Analysis & Probability Drill Sheets
CC3217	Grades 6-8 Five Strands of Math Big Book Drill Sheets
	PRINCIPLES & STANDARDS OF MATH SERIES
CC3300	Grades PK-2 Number & Operations Task & Drill Sheets
CC3301	Grades PK-2 Algebra Task & Drill Sheets
CC3302	Grades PK-2 Geometry Task & Drill Sheets
CC3303	Grades PK-2 Measurement Task & Drill Sheets
CC3304	Grades PK-2 Data Analysis & Probability Task & Drills
CC3306	Grades 3-5 Number & Operations Task & Drill Sheets
CC3307	Grades 3-5 Algebra Task & Drill Sheets
CC3308	Grades 3-5 Geometry Task & Drill Sheets
CC3309	Grades 3-5 Measurement Task & Drill Sheets
CC3310	Grades 3-5 Data Analysis & Probability Task & Drills
CC3312	Grades 6-8 Number & Operations Task & Drill Sheets
CC3313	Grades 6-8 Algebra Task & Drill Sheets
CC3314	Grades 6-8 Geometry Task & Drill Sheets
CC3315	Grades 6-8 Measurement Task & Drill Sheets
CC3316	Grades 6-8 Data Analysis & Probability Task & Drills